FINDING HUMAN

REVISED EDITION

J.D. GILL

CreateSpace 2014

God not only plays dice. He also some-
times throws the dice where they cannot be
seen.

--Stephen Hawking

CONTENTS

PART I

Joseph Campbell in his extensive reading of ancient mythology made the discovery that primitive people from widely different places told a similar story in their myths and legends. Campbell called this the monomyth (1949). This, he reasoned, was an essential human truth, the "song of the blood."

Since there was no way such disparate people could have communicated, the similarity of their stories pointed to something essentially human.

Campbell called the story "The Hero's Journey." This, he said, was essentially a journey from the factual world to the spirit world. It was a profoundly inner journey of transformation. The act of transformation made one into a different person.

Ever since I read *The Hero with a Thousand Faces* in my undergraduate career, I have always thought it a brilliant piece of work. And of course Campbell was a profound and engaging scholar.

But the title always bothered me.

The *hero*. Why have it be the hero? It did not even help when Campbell described the hero as: "The hero is the man of self achieved submission (1949, P. 16)."

To be fair Campbell was 1) male and 2) a student of mythology. Brilliant and widely read though he was, these truths remain.

Ours is an era of postmodernism. Here it is thought that what we may see is importantly and crucially influenced by where we stand. There is no uncontaminated context.

When I read these myths and stories, I also sensed the essential similarity in them. However the ways I found them to be similar were:

1. The journey is that of a *person* a human
   being (not necessarily a man).

2. The journey is always from a place that
   is known to a place that is beyond what is
   known.

3. This journey is accomplished by *surrendering* to the crossing despite the fear
   that such a crossing inspires.

Thus there is always what we know and what lies beyond what we know. And we have to do something with this situation. We can, for example, try to get into and experience that which is beyond what we know. We can build a wall and pretend that what we don't know is not there. We can try to get someone else to go, so we don't have to, &c. But we have to do something.

Campbell called this "the call to adventure." Actually it may happen in many ways. For example, what I know may not be working very well—or at all. I may have an unquenchable curiosity. I may be rebelling against a confining and abusive situation.

No matter what the impetus is, going beyond what I know is never easy. This is true for several reasons:

> 1. I was likely raised in a family unit. There I encountered an unconscious teaching concerning place. This family is where I belonged. I didn't belong across the street. With *those people*. It is dangerous to leave home. I might get lost, and terrible things could happen to me. I might not be able to find my way back, &c. Blood is blood, after all, and it would be improper for me to leave home—where I belong.

> 2. Historically, culture has been essentially tribal. This is my tribe. *Those people* are from a different tribe. They are *other*. The only way our tribe can survive is if we band together

and develop a unified front against incursions of other tribes who may seek to overpower us and take what we have. Over time, tribes became larger tribes and then city-states. City-states had to be strong to protect themselves from being taken over by other city-states. Countries developed national identities and sought to distinguish themselves from one another. The world's mythology may have similar essential themes, but the ways those themes are regionally or tribally inflected are different. The assumption is we belong to our tribe, city-state, or nation. We don't belong to *those* tribes, city-states, or nations.

3. Our neurobiology is programmed with basic survival mechanisms. For example, if one over-stimulates an infant, the infant will simply go to sleep. This is a primitive form of avoidance. Also, if I find myself lost or threatened, I will experience a "flight or fight" arousal. Here, blood drains out of the core and is pumped to the extremities in order to facilitate vigorous behavior.   Leaving what is known and safe for what is unknown and quite possibly unsafe will trigger the autonomic nervous system into an arousal state. This is experienced as *fear*. The fear is trying to keep me home and therefore, presumably, safe.

These phenomena may be observed on any playground. Children will go off by themselves to play, then they will return and touch mommy or daddy, and then go off again, &c. We go into the city and come back. We try to learn to tolerate incursions into the unknown.

But leaving home to fly all the way across the country to go to school for at least four years is different. No amount of excitement will block the fear in that.

Still, though these crossings are difficult and cost us so much anguish, there is a positive quality to them. That is, we get to see things from a different perspective. Thus, in postmodern terms, we are standing in a different place, and that contributes to our ability to see differently from how we could see when we were standing in our old place. *It is this difference in perspective that is the whole point.*

This is the case, because:

1. The old has become so usual, I have failed to attend to it with much acuity. That is, I pay less attention to the usual surround than I do to an entirely new one.

There is an old saying that the fish will be the last thing to discover the water. This is the case as the fish has not experienced anything like not water. The water can't be seen, because there is nothing with which it might be contrasted. (Contrast is required for seeing.)

2. An inside view and an outside view is never the same. Salt Lake City doesn't look the

same from Salt Lake City as it does from Rome. Again, contrast is required for seeing.

3. With the experience of many different "outsides," I begin to see that my original place, far from being how the world is, is really just one small facet of that world. Thus, Topeka, Kansas is really not the center of very much at all. Having experiences of what lies beyond, may make it so I find it difficult to return home, as I find it too confining there now.

When my son Anthony flew across the country to attend the University of Pennsylvania, he was very uncertain. Four years later when he graduated, the president of the university stood up, and she said:

> You people, having graduated from this institution, know something you could not possibly have known four or so years ago when you came here. You know what it is to have a college education—and now you know what everybody has been talking about.
>
> So go do something.

Then she sat down. I thought, "Damn!" They don't talk like that where I graduate. And then I thought: That's right

—that is precisely the point of psychoanalysis: you put yourself in a position (i.e., across the line) to have an experience that allows you to see from a different perspective, *and that changes everything!*

You now have an ability you would not have had if you had stayed home, avoided the fear of leaving, and been "safe."

Such experiences become *life changing events*. There are several including:

1. Getting a higher education.

2. Becoming a parent.

3. Falling in love.

4. Visiting foreign countries.

5. Experiencing depth psychotherapy or psychoanalysis.

6. Having a serious religious or transformative experience.

Each of these separates you from those who have not experienced such things—and the separation is *profound*. Furthermore, there is no other way to attain such awareness.

I submit to you, the dilemmas involved and the awareness that results from such experiences is what the essential human myths have been about—which is far more than a hero's journey to the spiritual world. That is actually a metaphor from prior generations that did not yet have the psychological acuity we have developed today.

That is to say, primitive preoccupation with Gods and transcendent explanations tended to focus thought in this direction and away from transformative experiences available apart from the spiritual, though not necessarily apart from the *sacred*. A child can be that.

Obviously, new developments will yield even better kinds of awareness and seeing from the newer positions where we stand.

PART II

I would like to illustrate the above position with two significant myths. The first is the Legend of the Holy Grail, and the second is the story of Eros and Psyche.

THE HOLY GRAIL

The Legend of the Holy Grail concerns the search for enlightenment. This is a very recent myth--as such things go. It dates from the twelfth century.

The Legend of the Holy Grail was first written as a poem by Chretien de Troyes, a French poet in the court of Eleanor of Aquitaine.

Twelfth Century Europe was a fairly dismal place. There was severe religious repression and a powerful pressure to fit in. In order to appear to fit, people were living inauthentic lives.

They worked at jobs they hated; they were in marriages with people they didn't love.

Everyone was pretending to be something he or she was not. This state of affairs produced an emotional condition known as the wasteland.

The question is how do you heal an inauthentic life?

The answer is by the emergence of an authentic life.

The myth is going to tell us that the essential requirement for the development of awareness is the individual quest for awareness. And further, that it is this individual awareness that is sacred--more than any group, more than any doctrine.

The story begins with the Grail Castle. The Grail Castle is in trouble. The King is wounded. Kings in medieval poems are always wounded. The Fisher King is wounded in the genitals and also wounded somewhere else. His wounds are severe, but he is incapable of dying, so he can only cry out and suffer all the time.

His kingdom has become fallow, nothing can grow, and no babies can be conceived. This, again, is the situation of the wasteland.

It is the wasteland as the ruler is impotent, and therefore the kingdom doesn't work. It is really the condition most of us experience--our kingdoms don't work either.

The Fisher King got wounded different ways in different accounts, but a good one is that he was off in the woods and was lost (woods are a symbol of the self). He was hungry and came upon a recently abandoned camp with a fish roasting on a spit. Quickly, he reached for a portion of the fish, but when he touched it, it burned his hand. He dropped the fish and put his fingers in his mouth to cool them--thus getting just a taste of the fish.

The Fisher King got his name because he was wounded by a fish. We may think of the fish as a symbol of his destiny, the significance of his life--but the Fisher King was too young and unprepared to grasp it, so he was wounded by it--still he did get a taste of it. Ever since then, he only can spend his time fishing, hoping to get back to what he needs to be--but he is sadly not up to the task.

(The fish is the creature from the water--it is the life that comes out of the unconscious.)

The Fisher King keeps his wound because he has not figured out that he is alienated from himself. He keeps trying to fix things externally. This is a "mature" approach, one permissible at court.

Another way to express this same thought is that the Fisher King is ill, because he did not earn his position by his own authenticity. He inherited it. Thus he has never uncovered his true self and is therefore impotent.

A similar image from Hindu is that of a light bulb covered with dust. One's true nature is the light and the dust is the teaching laid upon it. The wasteland is living in the dusty dark, and the sense of the vision quest is how to get back to the light.

It was thought the malaise caused by the impotent king could only be solved by a fool. The answer, that is, must come from outside--from the place least expected. Now to the fool.

In this blighted kingdom, there lived a woman, whose name was Heart Sorrow. Her husband and oldest sons had been killed in knighthood, and so she took the youngest-- whose name is Parsifal--which means simple fool--and went off to live in the country where the boy would not see any knights and therefore would not be tempted to join with them (she tries to shield him from his destiny and to keep him with her).

Parsifal is a real hick. The mother's crippling plan works beautifully until, one day, Parsifal is out playing and sees five knights riding past. Parsifal thinks they are gods in their splendid regalia and decides he must follow them. His mother is heartbroken upon hearing this news, but she knows she cannot retain him. She does, however, give him three pieces of advice.

(1) Respect all fair damsels.
(2) Go to church daily.
(3) Do not ask any questions.

This is matriarchal advice--and as we shall see gets the boy in all kinds of trouble.

Parsifal sets out. He is so naive, he has to ask the way to find the knights. This pure innocence, unharmed by training to be worldly or committed to points of view is the only thing that can touch the human heart (i.e., it is the higher forms, not the lower forms that are truly seductive). This instinctive, uninhibited, (foolish) purity is the world's only hope.

Parsifal has many adventures, most involving his botched attempts to deal with women. He is naive about the ways of women and treats them as his mother told him to, thereby getting nowhere.

Parsifal's first great encounter is with the Red Knight. This knight has completely overpowered King Arthur's court. The Red Knight is magnificent. He is dressed in crimson armor and has a jet black horse. Parsifal asks the Red Knight how he too can become a knight. The Red Knight laughingly tells him to go to King Arthur's court.

Parsifal senses no irony in this, and so he does go to Arthur's court. He asks the people there how to become a knight, and everyone laughs at him. He is brought to King Arthur himself who has a damsel (his daughter) with him who has not smiled in six years. Because of this there is a pall over the court. A legend (an input from the unconscious) said that she would laugh only when someone makes her laugh. No one has been able to accomplish this.

When Parsifal walks in, he trips over his feet and lands in the fire. The damsel bursts into laughter over the ridiculous appearance of this young fool. This impresses everyone.

Arthur, who can do nothing, but usually can see pretty well, realizes something big is going on here. He asks Parsifal what he can do for him, and Parsifal says he wants the Red Knight's armor.

King Arthur says that as a reward for freeing the damsel, and therefore the court and the kingdom, he will grant Parsifal this wish. He can have the armor: all he has to do is get it.

Parsifal senses no irony in this either, is happy, and goes to find the Red Knight. He finds him, challenges him, and in a crazy bout of original good luck, defeats him.

He takes off the armor and puts it on--but puts it on *over* his mother's homespun dress, which he has been wearing.

The point of the Red Knight is that he represents the realization of capacity and virility. In defeating him Parsifal overcomes his first big obstacle. This is to achieve, in other words, his own capability--essential for significance—a tempering of aggression into courage. But even so Parsifal still keeps to feminine rules underneath.

When he gets on the Red Knight's horse, it takes off, and he can't stop it (it is a dark horse, that is a creature of the unconscious). It leads him to Gournamond's castle.

Gournamond is the "male-mother." This is to be his mentor (Yoda), who teaches him to be a knight. Gournamond teaches Parsifal the only proper pursuit for a knight is the search for the Grail. Thus Gournamond is the teacher who urges Parsifal to breach the horizon. He also teaches two things (these are visionary things--as opposed to his mother's teachings):

(1) He is never to seduce nor be seduced by a woman.

(2) When he gets to the Grail Castle, he must ask the question: Whom does the Grail serve?

The sense of question (1) has to do with inner realities, not external ones. One must come to grips with one's nature. One is not to get out of balance and let the feminine or masculine side win out. A balance between the two, excluding neither, is the only adjustment that will work. This is to say the polarities must be balanced. Partial awareness or identification is insufficient.

Thus, following Gournamond's teaching, Parsifal goes off searching for the Grail by going in the direction of the middle, i.e., between the pairs of opposites (that is actually where the Grail is, because that is what it symbolizes: the unity world beyond the pairs of opposites).

This is absolutely to oppose the teachings of his mother.

The sense of question (2) is that of the meaning of the Grail itself. The chalice holds that which is poured into it. Thus the Grail is the container into which the higher forms pour meaning. In other words, the Grail has to do with the meaning of life. The question whom does the Grail serve is the same thing as asking what is the meaning of life (my life)? That is: who am I?

A balanced creature that understands who her she is, is the sense of a knight. This, in other words, is an authentic life. At this point Parsifal goes to visit his mother. He finds she has died of a broken heart. This is the destiny of mothers, to produce the forms that must abandon them, to be a vehicle of life itself.

Then Parsifal meets Blanche Fleur. He defeats her enemies and embraces her, but though they sleep together shoulder to shoulder, thigh to thigh, knee to knee, their embrace is chaste. She is his feminine side. Gournamond's instruction has to do with Blanche Fleur.

This is to bring one's feminine and masculine elements together—that is one's polarities—in a respectful embrace. They serve each other--they do not compete or take advantage of each other. They help each other. They are true friends.

After leaving Blanche Fleur, Parsifal travels on. He meets two men in a boat. It is the Fisher King, fishing, who invites him to his castle for dinner. This is the Grail Castle. Parsifal goes. At the celebration, a youth carries in a sword, which drips blood, and a maiden carries the Grail. Everyone drinks from the Grail, including Parsifal. He is given the sword by the Fisher King. But he listens to his mother's advice rather than to Gournamond, and does not ask the question. He thinks, "I will do it tomorrow." (Think of the doctor in the film The Field of Dreams who said, "I always thought there would be another day; I did not know that would be the only day.")

The boy doesn't ask the question because he doesn't believe in, nor act from his true self (he doesn't dare expose his real nature). He goes along with the social customs (and his mother's teachings) and does not seize his destiny. This is the essential wasteland condition, co-dependency. It is the failure to ask the dumb question in class.

Tomorrow is too late, the castle vanishes, and Parsifal is lost again in the woods and alone.

His ties to his mother have cost him the chance to stay in the Grail Castle. Only by overcoming the influence of his mother (that is, the advice to stay within the bounds of the imposed rules so others will like you), can Parsifal ever solve his quest and find the meaning of life.

The bleeding sword is a symbol of the destructive path. This is a true of a person afraid to come to suffering to get out of his impasse. Rather than conquering what is outside of him, he must suffer the pain of his true self. (The answer is not *out there*.)

Parsifal is essentially lost after the Grail Castle event. Most people he meets are women who recite all of his misdeeds and blame the malaise of the land on him. He failed to ask the question and therefore demonstrated he is another ineffectual male.

Still, because of the Grail Castle incident, it suddenly comes to Parsifal who he is. He has not known before that destiny equals identity.

Also the sword he has will break the first time he uses it. A maiden tells him (the oracle) that only when it is mended by the smith who made it will it last him the rest of his life. This means the sword of capability one gets from one's father is not sufficient. Only the sword that comes from the vision quest will not break.

Parsifal sees a falcon attack three geese and three drops three drops of blood fall on the snow. He remembers Blanche Fleur and rather than forging off on a self-decided direction for his quest, he surrenders to three knights who come riding along, one of whom is Gawain. They bring him back to Arthur's court. It seems Parsifal has become a legend in court due to all his victories (which have little to do with his quest).

The point of the quest, again and again, is to replace perfection with completeness. That which is excluded must become your enemy and defeat you. This is why conquering is never the answer. One can't conquer higher influence (destiny). This is also why Parsifal must not identify with only the male *or* female side. If he chooses to align himself with one or the other of the pairs of opposites, the quest will fail.

Parsifal is received as the greatest knight at Arthur's court. A huge feast is offered. This symbolizes the apex of one's career, the pinnacle of capability in the lower sense (i.e., the outer world.)

At the height of the celebration, a hideous damsel rides in from the woods and into court on a diseased and crippled donkey. She recites each of Parsifal's sins. "It is all your fault," she says. Parsifal has not asked the question and therefore, *because of him*, the wasteland remains, despite the revalry, honor, and celebration of the day.

She stops the feast and sends all the knights on a quest. She sends Parsifal off for the second time to find the Grail Castle—and this time to ask the question.

The hag is the dark part of feminine side of the unconscious (this is the witch). She is the voice inside which reminds you of your destiny. She is hideous, as indeed all creatures from the unconscious and dreams seem to be strange or even weird (remember the film *Never Ending Story)*.

She knows Parsifal's sins, because she experiences the problems caused by the failures of the knights who are caught up only in self focused activities and revelries.

Parsifal goes off again on his quest—remember Parsifal is a fool who is not completely trained in the ways of this world, and therefore not completely of it (he is the influence from without). He is the only knight who is able to find the Grail, because he is the only one who has enough sense to lay the horse's reins down on the horse's neck.

Joseph Campbell said of true knighthood:

To go on a quest, it was thought to be a disgrace to go forth in a group, so each was to enter the forest at the point he himself had chosen, where it was darkest and there was no path (1990, p 211).

(Gurus, his mother, the authorities of society, on the other hand, know the path for you -- which is actually what created the wasteland in the first place and got you lost).

This is Parsifal's unique gift. He alone is able to surrender to the guiding rhythms of eternity. Thus he alone can be guided by eternity to an answer from beyond.

At this point Parsifal has many, many different kinds of adventures with men and women, and as usual, he gets lost and forgets his pursuit. Years pass. He forgets about Blanche Fleur who represents his feminine side. He is "conquering more and enjoying it less."

One day, he comes upon a group of true pilgrims who are on the road. They say to him, "Why are you riding around, dressed in armor on Good Friday?"

Parsifal suddenly remembers his destiny. He remembers about the quest; he remembers Blanche Fleur. He is stricken with nostalgia and remorse.

"Where are you going?" he asks them.

"We are going to visit the hermit who lives in the woods for Good Friday confession," they reply.

Parsifal joins in and goes with them. (This represents his sudden realization that he can't work through his dilemma in the external world. No external solution will make a difference in his life at this point.)

The hermit in the woods is the masculine side of the unconscious. (Remember the Hermit from the Tarot cards—this is the person who has found a way to wisdom beyond the physical world, which, incidentally, echoes the fourth stage of Hindu development).

When the hermit sees Parsifal, he immediately begins, of course, to recite all Parsifal's sins (he knows when you are sleeping; he knows when you are awake)—and by now this is a long list!

The Hermit tells Parsifal it is because of his mother this has happened to him. His mother tie has prevented him from finding the Grail Castle and freeing it from its spell. *He has not been able to treat his mother properly, because he has not been able to free himself from her and realize his own self (i.e., he is still inauthentic).* Parsifal has yet to genuinely leave home, the known place.

The Hermit gives Parsifal absolution and tells him he must immediately go to the Grail Castle. At this point Parsifal is free to make his own clear way to the Grail Castle, which he does immediately.

At this point the poem of Chretien stops.

There are many endings written for it. Joseph Campbell wondered if Chretien, who was a Christian, didn't like where the poem was pointing and "quit while he was ahead."

In one sense, however, it is a lovely place for the poem to end. It is an extremely feminine literary ending.

Ending here, the poem says the way to become enlightened is to go on a vision quest, beyond the known, profane world--that this quest is to be guided by the unconscious in order to reach a greater truth.

The purpose of enlightenment is to answer the question "Who am I?"

Further, in a profoundly fundamental way, this effort is essential for life itself. Without it, life would simply not be possible.

In the Greek way of putting it, this sort of vision is the "seed" that is essential for the life of the human soul, and that without a human soul, persons would not be truly human.

Also, ending the tale here begs you to complete it with your own inflection, your own sense of the vision (the result of your own solitary experience in the woods).

Probably the most inspired ending has Parsifal going directly to the Grail Castle. Suddenly he is aware he has always known exactly where it is. He crosses the same drawbridge, and the Fisher King is still suffering, the land is still fallow. The Grail Keeper brings out the Grail, and this time Parsifal asks the question: "Whom does the Grail Serve?"

The answer that is given is: "The Grail serves the Grail King."

What an amazing answer!

All this capacity, all this immense achievement is ultimately not for oneself alone—it is in the service of life and awareness.

The Grail King is the transcendent counterpart of the Fisher King. True life is always beyond the lower forms and matter.

As soon as Parsifal asks the question, the Fisher King is healed, the kingdom becomes productive, the women all get pregnant, &c.

What makes life work is awareness that comes from a different kind of experience. The point of the Grail story is that it is the individual who is divine, not the social rules. Parsifal fails when he does what he is told rather than following his own heart. (He listened to Kings 2:15).

The Grail message is significant for the 12th Century, a time when life was basically artificial and inauthentic—when the teachings of the church had imposed a rigid pattern or code on life—to be followed or else!!!

The poem is saying the courage to move beyond the "fit in and follow or else" mentality is the answer for *life*. Life needs it—we need it. Without such courage, we are doomed to the Dark Ages.

Symbolically, the grail is the earthly vessel into which the essence of expanded truth can be poured. The vessel *contains* this truth. This is the sense of life; it is the vessel for human awareness.

It is, through life-consuming effort of transformation the miracle of the birth of light of awareness is realized.

The story is saying the object of life is not personal achievement or happiness, but serving the Grail, that is awareness. The realization of this truth alone brings about the ability to come to peace —which heals the Fisher King.

EROS AND PSYCHE

The myth of Eros and Psyche concerns the search for love. This myth comes from Ancient Greece and is a much more powerful myth than the Holy Grail. It concerns the relative sectors of the known and the beyond--and how to move from the first to the second.

Psyche is a human being who is the most beautiful creature on earth. She has two terrible sisters (the prototype of the Cinderella story).

Being so amazingly beautiful, Psyche is worshiped as if she were Aphrodite herself (Aphrodite is the Goddess of

Love). This is a mortal threat to Aphrodite. It means beauty alone is enough, that heaven is irrelevant. Aphrodite's temples fall to ruin, because people flock to Psyche rather than to the temples. Essentially the center has moved from heaven to earth.

Thus mortal beauty is worshiped rather than the divine.

This is not much of a consolation to Psyche, however, because she is *worshiped* but not *loved* (no one does anything). She has no joy in her loveliness (limited dimensions cannot bring joy or transcendence).

Aphrodite cooks up plan to get rid of Psyche. She gets her son, Eros God of Love, no less, to go to earth and smite Psyche with an incurable passion for the vilest of creatures.

Meanwhile, Psyche's sisters marry kings and are busy manipulating them out of their treasures—which seems to be the epitome of material mentality.

In despair, Psyche's father consults the oracle at Delphi (Apollo's oracle) and is told Psyche is to be led out to a rocky crag and abandoned to marry the rock monster.

Here the rock monster is a creature from beyond. Psyche's destiny, in other words, is to be different from her sisters.

The wedding is changed to a funeral of sorts. The wedding/funeral procession illustrates the loss of the past and the birth of the new life, which is symbolized by a wedding.

This act, which in Greece is known as the "Rape of Persephone," involves the separation of the mother and the daughter, that is the triumph of new life over the old.

Seen as a victory for males, such an act is a death and resurrection for the female: she changes from being a flower maiden to a fruit woman.

Psyche is left out on the rocky crag to await her fate. Hers is the death of the psychological virginity, that is the retention of the self. It is a basic surrender.

As Psyche is shivering on her rocky crag, soft winds appear and lift her to a pleasure bower in the woods. At evening an unknown lover appears and makes her his bride. (It is Eros, unbeknownst to Psyche). He tells her he will continue to be her lover as long as she does not look upon him, that is she does not know him.

Psyche, in time, learns to love her husband (as yet unseen). This goes on a long time, and Psyche is satisfied.

As you might imagine there are many interpretations of this portion of the myth. It is likely *not* an account of patriarchal over-control of women, but rather the surrender on Psyche's part to what she could not yet comprehend (Eros is a God but Psyche is mortal).

Her husband tells her she can't know him, because she can't. She does not have enough preparation. She only knows earthly things. Psyche, in other words, doesn't have a sophisticated enough base to interpret the data. From her position, she would miss the point.

That is, her "knowing" at this point would not be metaphorical. It would still be based in the facts.

Psyche eventually grows lonely for her home and longs to see her worthless sisters again. She wants to invite them to visit her.

Eros warns her not to listen to her sisters, especially if they inquire as to what her husband is like (as they no doubt will do). Psyche is happy to agree.

Psyche's wish represents a regressive pull back to the family, that part of the self that feels beholden to one's home.

The sisters visit the pleasure bower and are *green* with envy. Their younger sister has out-done them. They immediately try to trash her good fortune and ask her about her husband.

Psyche makes up a story, but the sisters realize the ruse— they are afraid Psyche will be a goddess.

Eros warns her again, more urgently.

> "Do you see," he said, "what great peril you are in?...Those false she wolves are weaving some deep plot of sin against you, whose purpose is this: to persuade you to seek to

35

know my face, which, as I have told you, if you once see, you will see no more. And so if hereafter those wicked ghouls come hither armed with their dark designs—and they will come, that I know--speak not at all with them, or of your simple unsuspecting soul is too tender to endure that, at least neither give ear nor utterance to anything concerning your husband. For soon we shall have issue, and even now your womb, a child's as yet, beats a child like to you. If you keep my secret in silence, he shall be a God; if you divulge it, a mortal."

This is the tug of war between heaven and earth, represented in the agony of Jesus as well as the grandstand scene in the film *The Field of Dreams*. It is the conflict between what is known and what lies beyond what is known.

The child that Psyche is carrying is a spiritual child, that is an awareness. This is the "higher pregnancy" of Eleusis. If Psyche follows a divine path, the child will be spiritual; if she follows a lower path, mortal.

Psyche assures Eros she can handle her sisters, and they return.

By manipulation the sisters attempt to bring Psyche back into the family circle, which she has disgraced by joining with a man of unknown power.

They say:

"Ah! you are happy, for you live in blessed ignorance of your evil plight and have no suspicion of your peril. But we cannot sleep for the care with which we watch over your happiness and are torn with anguish for your misfortunes. For we have learned the truth....He that lies secretly by your side at night is a huge serpent with a thousand tangled coils; blood and deadly poison drip from his throat and from the cavernous horror of his gaping maw...you will not much longer feast on such dainties or receive such loving service, but so soon as your time has come, he will devour you with the ripe fruit of your womb. The hour has come when you must choose whether to believe your sisters, whose sole care is for your dear safety, to flee from death and live with us, free from all thought of peril, or find a grave in the entrails of a cruel monster. If the musical solitude of this fair landscape, if the joys of your secret love still delight you, and you are content to lie in the embraces of a foul and venomous snake, at least we, your loving sisters, have done our duty."

This may be thought of as the family's view of men.

The sisters cook up a plot. Psyche is to hide a lamp and a knife under the bed, and when her husband has fallen asleep, she is to shine the light on him, look at him, and cut off his head. Then she will be safe and can go live with her sisters.

The sisters leave. Eros returns. There ensues a long period of tender lovemaking (Eros is good at this). He falls asleep. Psyche seizes the moment. She lights the lamp, creeps around the bed, and gazes upon him.

To her amazement it is not a serpent but Eros himself, the God of love! She drops the knife and pricks her finger on one of his arrows, thus falling deeply in love with him--but in her overwhelmed state, her hand trembles, and a drop of burning oil falls on Eros' shoulder, burning him.

He wakes, is outraged by her betrayal, and begins to fly off. Psyche, in desperation, grasps his legs and manages to hang on just until they have cleared the boundaries of paradise. Then she falls to earth--barefoot and pregnant in the world that has now become forever alien to her.

It is of course the case Psyche cannot remain in the darkness of blind pleasure. She must come to her own awareness, that is the realization of her true, individual self—beyond the rules into which she has been raised to fit.

When she gazes on Eros (1) her seizing of awareness wounds him (2) she sees he is a God, that is she sees eternity *through him* for the first time (3) she plunges herself into a loneliness which is almost unendurable.

The pricking of the self with the arrow amounts to a deflowering in the sense that she has joined with the world beyond. She sees eternity and is not destroyed; her love opens to eternity.

This is a profound sort of religious transformation. The myth is saying that the experience of love is a form of religious transformation.

With Eros gone, Psyche must discover her "self." This she must discover herself not as a reflection of the world of women, not as reflection of the world of men, but her true self.

The point is: through her experience of Eros (the divine principle of love), she is able to see beyond the present to the eternal.

It is at this point Psyche enters on her own tragic destiny (her own psychotherapy, we might say).

Psyche's act ends the age of dominance by the Gods alone and begins an age of human love. That is, she becomes a new sort of Aphrodite.

Psyche's task is to bring Eros to her area (to human life) from the region of the Gods. *In this sense*, Aphrodite becomes the enemy.

Following the above experience, Psyche is destitute. She decides to kill herself and throws herself in the river (that is in the unconscious--the river Styx), but the river won't have her and throws her back.

On the shore the distraught Psyche meets Pan. Pan was the son of Hermes and was not fully human (he had the feet and torso of a goat). Pan was a great musician, however, second only to Apollo himself (music, like poetry was the language of the heart). Pan could seduce the nymphs with his pipes made from the river reeds (the material of the fertile earth, that is life itself), but he was always rejected by them, because he was ugly. He liked to hang out by rivers where, upon hearing his music, one was seized by "pan-ic" which was a state *highly prized* by the ancients. It meant the orderly, earthly ground was going to be intruded upon by the divine. Also, Pan knew all about unrequited love.

Pan provides the answer for the myth. He diagnoses the condition and prescribes the cure. This is the most important utterance in the tale.

He says,

> "Fair maiden, I am but a rude rustic shepherd, but long old age and ripe experience have taught me much. If I guess rightly (though men that are wise call it no guess, but rather divination), your weak and tottering steps, your body's exceeding pallor, your unceasing sighs, and still more your mournful eyes, tell me that you are faint from excess of love. Wherefore give ear to me and seek no more to slay yourself by casting yourself headlong down, nor by any manner of self-slaughter. Cease from your grief and lay aside your sorrow, and rather

address Eros, the mightiest of Gods, with fervent prayer and win him by tender submission, for he is an amorous and softhearted youth."

Thus Pan, who is part human and part divine and thus the connection between the two, tells Psyche: of all the solutions she might pursue, love is the answer.

This sets the direction for the tale.

Eros, meanwhile, goes home, ill with his wound (the same wound his mother has, the limited mortal desecration of the divine). Aphrodite is furious when she finds out the upstart broad has also wounded her son.

Psyche finds her way to Demeter's temple at Eleusis. This is the most important temple in antiquity. Demeter is the goddess of the earth (her name is Ceres in Roman, from which we get the word "cereal"). She is the Goddess of fertility, pregnancy, and all things female in the human or life sense. Her rites also provide the method of crossing from the factual to the transcendent.

Demeter tells Psyche to keep going (i.e., refuses her shelter). She tells Psyche that Aphrodite "...has a good heart after all..." "And so you must leave my temple without more ado and count it for the best that I have not kept you here, nor given you my protection."

Demeter realizes that fertility is not Psyche's problem (she is, rather, on a quest to realize love).

So Psyche takes a baby step toward the divine and visits the temple of Hera, Zeus' wife--who controls domestic affairs in heaven. Hera also cannot help her and sends her to Aphrodite.

At this point Psyche gets even with her sisters by promising them riches--which ultimately lead to the deaths of both sisters.

Then she is truly alone. All hope is lost. Only at this point, can she submit to the will of eternity. This is, of course, the solution to the Oedipus complex. The realization that reality, not your own fantasies, will decide your life.

When Psyche abandons the attempt to do it all her way, she *must* call upon Aphrodite for help (i.e., "higher" or instinctive guidance). Only then can she surrender to her "certain death." It is the only hope she has for reuniting with Eros. Her hopes shattered, there is no way for her to solve the dilemma on her own.

When Psyche appears before Aphrodite at last, Aphrodite says, "So at last you have come to understand who is your mistress, you worthless slut."

Aphrodite has been threatened to the core of her being by Psyche. Psyche is practicing medicine without a license.

Psyche surrenders *everything* and asks for Aphrodite's help. This is an act of turning in complete humiliation to her greatest enemy. It is the only thing she has left.

I am reminded of Joseph Campbell's rule: "when you are falling, dive."

Psyche surrenders to eternity. This is her twelve step program.

Aphrodite gives Psyche four famous, and utterly impossible, tasks to perform. This resembles the twelve tasks of Hercules, the struggle of the Greek consciousness for mastery over raw, animalistic nature and the development of higher consciousness (the nine tones and muses which lead from Thalia to the very throne of Apollo).

TASK 1

For the first task, Aphrodite shows Psyche a room with a huge pile of seeds--of all kinds. "I'm going to a wedding," says Aphrodite, "Sort these all out in like-seeded piles by sundown when I will return." Then she leaves.

Psyche is overwhelmed by the impossibility of sorting millions of seeds, sits down, and thinks of killing herself (she always thinks this when she hears of the next step)-- actually it is not a bad idea-- it's just that she hasn't figured out what needs to die (the old life).

While Psyche is despairing, an army of ants comes in to help her. The ants quickly take on the task and in no time have the seeds all sorted into their individual piles.

What is happening here? The particularly feminine way to solve a problem is to go deep into the resting part of the self and wait for something to happen--rather than going out and making something happen, as the masculine does.

This is always the first task: sorting. You must be able to sort out what is important and find a way to respond to life in a prioritized fashion. The seeds are the masculine elements of the feminine earth. They are the potential of what can happen.

The ants are the instinctive creatures from the dark underworld or the unconscious. The task is solved, the tale is saying, by the instinctual world. It is the *instincts* which are able to sort through potentials and bring a focus to diffuse awareness.

Further, it is thought *feminine awareness is diffuse*--it responds to whatever needs there are. *Masculine awareness is focused*. The tale is saying Psyche's task is to develop some masculine qualities in her awareness.

She is able to respond to the tasks of Aphrodite, because she had been focused by Pan. He opened her eyes to the meaning in Aphrodite's seemingly senseless tasks. Psyche does these things because she realizes they are ultimately a way to Eros.

Aphrodite returns and is amazed. She thinks Psyche has cheated.

Next morning Aphrodite sends Psyche off on her second task.

TASK TWO

The second task is to bring back a handful of fleece from the golden rams

Again, Psyche is overwhelmed. She goes to the river and sees the golden rams out in the meadow. She immediately thinks of killing herself, and then tries to talk herself into solving the task.

This time it is the river reeds who come to her rescue. The river reeds are the fruit of the earth. They represent the voice of the earth because they can sing. They also grow next to and are nourished by the unconscious (water). Pan played music on a pipe made from the reeds of the earth which means this is the fundamental music of life.

The reeds tell her the sun heats up the gold, and if she were to touch it, she would be burned horribly. The thing to do, they say, is to wait until the sun goes down--then you can go along where the rams have been and pick the wool from the branches.

This is my favorite part of the myth. It is the pure aware sensibility in action. Psyche gets what she needs at no cost to anyone else. It is an elegant insight.

The point is you cannot confront power head on--or you will be destroyed by it. It is masculine spiritual power in this case, but it need not be. *Power* need not be confronted.

In fact is it is typically stupid to do so. The reeds whisper vegetative wisdom: wait, be patient, things change. This is the wisdom of growth.

If Psyche strove to confront the rams directly, she would be destroyed. But at nightfall, when the heat of the sun returns to the coolness of the moon, the "fruitful seed of light" may be found says Neumann. In other words, the solution is not to struggle, but to set up a fruitful contact between competing forces.

The first two tasks assigned to Psyche by Aphrodite require the development of (1) a trust in the fundamental truths of life, and (2) a successful method for dealing with power. By the time Psyche has completed these two tasks, she is quite a different creature from the one who only lived in the dark bliss of sexual pleasure.

Also, by being able to complete these tasks, there begins to be a secret sympathy between Aphrodite and Psyche. Psyche is developing the capacity of the higher awareness, which is what Aphrodite has, rather than staying in the factual world of her sisters.

TASK THREE

These previous preparatory tasks accomplished, Aphrodite sends Psyche off to get a vial of pure water from the Stygian waterfall.

This is the waterfall that feeds the river Styx (the river of forgetfulness) and Cocytus (the river of lamentation). These are the rivers of the underworld. The waterfall flows from high mountain crags.

The waterfall may be thought of as the uroboric symbol of the great unconscious element which links the upper and lower worlds together. This is the essential tie between the world of spirit and that of the earth. Psyche needs a portion of this quality just as she needs a portion of the power of the rams and the earth wisdom of the ants.

The waterfall cannot be approached, because it is guarded by serpents and surrounded by slippery rocks that deny traction. The point is no creature of the earth may contain it. (Psyche is a creature of the earth). Psyche sits on a rock in despair and thinks of killing herself, but she already knows the stream won't have her.

This time the riddle is solved when an eagle, symbol of Zeus himself, flies down to help her. The eagle takes the vial and easily flies above the slippery rocks and serpents to fill the vial.

Again, the meaning of this is profound. The water is the essential water of life. It is the stuff which links the world of the earth to the world of the spirit.

This is the water of *all* of life, not just the part only known by the Gods who live in Olympus--or Psyche's sisters who stayed in the matriarchy, ignorant of the higher regions.

The tale is saying that Psyche needs only a small portion of the divine connection. She, if you will, needs to possess a small portion of the divine link. She need not become divine herself.

Yet, the essence of the stream symbol is that it cannot be contained. Who can contain life? Psyche, in other words-- as vessel, is to give form and rest to that which is restless and flowing. This is to give form to life.

The river is the energy of the unconscious that Psyche must contain without being broken by it. She cannot do it herself (being of the earth--which Aphrodite knew).

That Zeus himself steps in and helps is also one of the most significant elements of the myth. Why did he do this?

Psyche's amazing quest, from her initial enlightenment, through a devoted journey, her willingness to surrender *everything*, and her transforming development through earlier tasks (*all of which have brought her away from the physical world and closer to the world of the transcendent--close enough for the Gods to notice her*), all this has earned the celebration of Zeus himself who is the most important God.

Now, for the first time, life may respond to Psyche as a complete being (because that is what she has become), rather than simply one of the girls.

Psyche now, is the field. No one else is.

Think: Zeus would not have given the time of day to any of Psyche's sisters. The third task of Psyche is the key to the question: how to make Zeus himself respond?

This requires the development of enough capacity that you can genuinely understand spirituality--while at the same time still not give up your attachment to the earth. Then you will be the one the eagle will help.

If you don't develop these qualities, you will die in the darkness of the earth.

Another important point is that Zeus is also Eros' father. (It is hard to know how this could be so, as Eros is the oldest and the youngest of the gods--he is born anew for each person--and was universally feared among heaven and earth for the enormous power of his arrows.

Zeus was no fan of Aphrodite's domination of Eros, and was, therefore, upset that Aphrodite had locked *his* ailing son in *her* back room, because she was furious at his dalliance with Psyche. By helping Psyche, he was helping Eros.

When Psyche has completed the third task, she is able to communicate directly with the spirit world. This is a powerful achievement.

With the third task complete, the resulting male-female spirituality of Psyche is evident. *In one act, she receives like the feminine, but, at the same time apprehends and knows like the masculine.*

From this vantage point, it can be seen that Eros disappeared precisely because Psyche's lamp could not recognize him for what he really is.

The three tasks she has endured were needed to develop the capacity to reveal him. That is, Psyche could not have known him before as she did not yet have the *base* in terms of which she could make a reasonable interpretation. The base required, quite different from the one she developed in the matriarchy, consists of three experiential parts: (1) managing fecundity, (2) dealing with powerful radiance, (3) containing the dynamic power of life.

In the beginning of the tale Psyche lived in darkness. Her lamp brought her the beginning of knowledge, the awareness of opposites (the fall in the garden). The coming of light (Logos awareness) made Eros visible.

Psyche does, in other words, what Aphrodite thought impossible. She develops higher courage and sensibility. In this sense, Psyche has become Christ. In *her* the worlds meet. In all major ancient religions, this kind of juncture is always divine--as it was in Greece.

TASK FOUR

The fourth task is that Aphrodite sends Psyche to Hades (the underworld) to bring back from Persephone, queen of the underworld, a small casket containing a portion of her beauty--just enough for the space of a single day.

Persephone is Demeter's daughter who was carried off to the underworld by Pluto (Hades). She ate a pomegranate seed with him, thus, according to Greek custom, making it impossible for her to return. This capture is often called the "Rape of Persephone." She is able to return only once a year to visit the earth. She brings her beauty with her at that time. And it is quite a glorious return: the springtime.

The beauty of Persephone is the beauty of the springtime, the full flowering of life. There is simply no beauty equal to it in the world.

The "Rape of Persephone" symbolizes the trouble caused when the male steals the daughter away from the mother-- and therefore creates a breach of the matriarchate by its arch enemy no less: the male. It is a fact known across centuries that this wound *never* closes.

Demeter could never let it go, and Demeter is a Goddess! Psyche goes to a tower and thinks of throwing herself off of it, but the tower gives her the instructions necessary for the completion of the task.

The tower is the symbol of civilization. That is, Psyche needs human knowledge of the symbols to solve the task. From the tower's knowledge, she learns she is to place two gold coins in her mouth and take two cakes of barley in her hands. When she gets to the entranceway to the lower regions, she will find the passage guarded by Cerberus, the three headed beast. One head is that of a lion, which symbolizes pride, one is that of a dog, which symbolizes desire, and one is that of a wolf, which symbolizes fear (the past which tears away what you have).

These are the human emotions that block the path. These are also precisely the emotions the Buddha had to overcome to find a solution for suffering.

Psyche is to give one of the cakes to Cerberus, and while the heads are arguing about who will eat it, she is to slip past.

She will meet a blind and lame man on the road, whose donkey has dropped its load of sticks. The man sells these sticks for survival. She is not to help this man.

When she gets to the river, Styx in this case--which surrounds the lower region--she is to let the ferryman take one of the coins from her mouth as payment for the journey across. Midway in the journey, a drowning man will reach for her in his last attempts to stay alive. She is to ignore this man. When she gets to the other side she will confront three women who are weaving the fabric of fate. Their yarn has become hopelessly entangled so they cannot progress. She is not to help them.

When she gets to Persephone's palace, she is to not eat with her, but only beg enough to sustain her. (To eat is to belong.) Psyche actually sits on the floor, not at the table and only begs a few grains of bread and water (this is the sacrament), no real food.

Then she is to follow these same instructions on her return trip--and deliver the casket to Aphrodite without opening it.

Psyche is able to follow the directions and completes the journey.

What does it mean?

The first three tasks were solved by "helpers," i.e., the inner powers reflected in Psyche's consciousness. The fourth, she must solve entirely by herself.

In the first three tasks, Psyche wrestled with the life principle. Here, she is placed in a direct struggle with death and transformation. Thus Psyche herself is asked to be the connecting link or bridge between these two aspects. Just as in task three she went to the highest heights for the solution, now she must go to the lowest depths.

To achieve the task: Psyche must be able to learn from the civilized culture, that is develop philosophical wisdom. Then she must then be able to surrender to the unconscious to guide the way, that is follow the Buddha.

The journey resembles the mysteries at Eleusis. There, barley was the symbol of Demeter. The secret of the grain is that it is cut and planted (donated to the underworld) in order to produce new life. The mysteries at Eleusis (the most important religious experience in ancient Greece) gave one an experience of the descent into death as the answer to eternal rebirth. This is Psyche's task.

The task also resembles Greek funeral rites. The dead were ferried across the river of forgetfulness to the underworld. This is why Psyche must not hand the coin to the ferry man herself (he would realize that she was not dead and was an impostor). People were buried in ancient Greece with *one* coin in their mouths to be given to the ferryman for the crossing. Psyche is asked to journey to death itself and return. This is quite a task.

She is not to help the lame man nor the drowning man.

It is thought feminine consciousness is diffuse. It's concern is *relatedness*. Thus it is (1) available for need when it arises (2) susceptible to pity ahead of concentration.

Masculine consciousness, on the other hand, is *focused*. Masculine consciousness can walk past and ignore the kitchen garbage repeatedly if that is not the task upon which it is focused.

Psyche, in addition to her relatedness abilities, is to develop a focused consciousness (that is, become a whole person). This, Aphrodite is quite sure, she cannot do. In other words, Psyche is to struggle against polarized nature itself.

The three women weaving fate are to be resisted because one must not weave one's fate, in other words don't do it your way. Especially don't mold the lives of children. They are not your children anyway; they are life's children. (This helps Psyche treat herself differently than her own mother treated her.)

Actually, with the solution to the fourth task, Psyche is able to replace her original sisters (remember them, the ones with the right fashions) with Aphrodite and Persephone—eternal sisters.

Psyche is able to accomplish all of this, which has required she transcend the boundaries of life in order to journey to the region of death itself, thus transcending the limits of the mortal. Psyche, that is to say, has journeyed through the eternal regions *by her own abilities*.

She is quite a capable person when she returns with the treasure and sits on a rock by the stream to rest, having attained the sunlight and the earth again.

Were the tale to end here, Psyche would have become like Athena: all talented and all powerful. But, remember, this is not Psyche's mission.

Her dream is to be reunited with Eros.

Seated on the rock, Psyche thinks, "The beauty of the springtime, eh? (every woman's desire)." "Why should Aphrodite get this--especially at my expense?" "Eros would surely not be able to resist me if I had the beauty of the springtime."

With thoughts like these, Psyche betrays the instructions and opens the casket. She immediately falls into an eternal "deathlike" sleep (the Stygian sleep).

This is the deathlike sleep of Kore, the barren, frigid beauty of maidenhood, without love of another, which is the goal of the matriarchate. This involves natural perfection without fate, suffering, or knowledge. (Sleeping beauty).

The threat in the fourth task is the seduction of narcissism (falling away from Eros and a return to the narcissistic love of the self).

The plan, however, isn't able to work. Psyche is not able to be drawn back into the matriarchate. Why?

She is pregnant.

This is *not* a pregnancy of nature, but of the fire of the individual soul itself.

The lower pregnancy unites mother and daughter in a common experience. The higher pregnancy (divine awareness brought on by the seed of light) unites the human psyche with the divine Eros.

In other words, the lower pregnancy can be accomplished at home. The higher pregnancy is the result of an infusion of that which lies beyond what is known. Psyche cannot be reclaimed by the matriarchate because part of her is now a part of what lies beyond, or the divine.

She originally gave up her blissful lovers' paradise to follow the agony of spiritual development-- out of blindness. Now she gives up remaining in the world beyond what we know, eternity, in order to remain a human (albeit aware) being.

What does this mean?

Psyche no longer wishes to exist for herself, nor for the matriarchate, but for Eros alone, and for no one else.

Two things happen:

First, by remaining for Eros, she earns the forgiveness of Aphrodite-Persephone (throwing all away for a man pleases Aphrodite to no end).

Second, through her more than heroic choice, she heals Eros and empowers him. That is, she arranges for him to fix the dilemma, rather than her.

By opening the box, she dies for Eros, which is a divine sacrifice. She gives herself and (as Neumann puts it) "...everything she has acquired for him."

This is not the naive act of a maiden, but an act of developed awareness. It is the essential feminine mystery (the vital feminine power): rebirth through love. It is precisely this act that is superior to the act of any Goddess.

Eros is mystically rendered whole by Psyche's action and immediately comes to her. He wipes the sleep from her eyes, wakes her with a kiss, and tells her to take the casket to Aphrodite as if nothing has happened.

Then he goes to his father, Zeus, and asks him to *announce* the marriage of Psyche and himself in heaven.

Zeus consults with the gods, and the marriage is arranged by his bidding.

A child is born, and her name is Joy (Rapture). This means that the true marriage is something that is accomplished in the heart, not at the altar.

Zeus invites the couple to live in Olympus (Psyche is the *only* mortal ever to be elevated to the status of a Goddess). Zeus did this because he realized that what Psyche had done was divine. Her actions were equal to anything the Gods had done.

The child that is born is also divine--and the child is a girl. What this signifies is that the supreme accomplishment of love is to bring joy to the world. The child also represents Psyche's secret inner loyalty to Eros.

———

It may be seen that in both these myths the goal is attained by surrendering to the task that presents itself and by giving up control. Parsifal had to lay the reins down on the horse's neck, and Psyche had to face Aphrodite.

Both of these myths involve a profound leaving. In both cases the dilemma could not be solved by staying at home or in one's usual place. Thus both involve finding a way to put oneself in position to have an entirely different sort of experience.

The task and the procedure are seen to be the same regardless of what the new life is. Routinely in ancient societies that which is beyond what is known is talked about in spiritual terms. But the life beyond what is known needn't be spiritual. It simply must be that which lies beyond what is known.

The ancients were drawn to spirituality in part as they were interested in cosmology. They wanted an explanation of who they were. Survival was a central concern. An ancient person was in danger from huge forces beyond him or her. An ancient person, for example, was no match for weather or disease.

Further, psychological projections were common. Dangerous creatures were thought to live in the mist. These creatures snatched and ate one's children. It did not occur to these people the creatures were personifications of their own fears.

It was in Ancient Greece that the forces beyond were thought of in human terms. At that point, the struggle was with forces within rather than with forces from without. One was asked to come to grips with what one did not know about oneself.

Coming to grips with that which lies beyond what is known is far more important in our time as our world is rapidly becoming one in which disparate elements, nations, or tribes must interact. Getting along with others requires abilities to sensibly deal with what is other.

It is not strange that what is other must be brought into the area of what is known before any meaningful dealings with it are possible. This is to say, we are rapidly entering a world where a primary focus must be on what lies beyond what we know.

PART III

It is fair to ask what relevance ancient myths might have for our lives today. Our world is vastly different from the time these myths were circulating. We as people are different. We have been raised in utterly different contexts, and our understanding of the world, especially that gained through scientific exploration, is far greater than it was for ancient people.

Each age sees through its own lens. Modern western cultures exist in an information age. This has shifted the focus toward technology. The speed of development in modern cultures renders advancements obsolete in increasingly short periods.

Feminism has played an outsized role in shifting notions of gender and social roles. Long cast into the status of underdogs, women have been increasingly freed in our time to discover their own identities. This, in turn, has been a stimulus for an increased focus on the self, its formulation, its problems, and its understanding.

There is a significant difference between one's gender *identity* (who one experiences oneself to be) and one's gender *role* (the gendered behavior one exhibits). There is also a difference between identity and sex, the latter of which is physical. Both gender identity and role have undergone sweeping changes. No longer are women necessarily identified with an identity dependent on and subservient to men. Women are, rather, increasingly encouraged to find their own destiny according to their own abilities and understandings of who they are.

Evidence for this is clear in the rapid increase in the numbers of women attaining advanced degrees from universities. Now common in professional ranks, women have become important figures in several fields once thought the province of men only.

It is no longer the case that women must choose between a career and having a family. It is increasingly common to find women who are able to excel at both. In possession of reproductive technology they are able to control, women are no longer slaves to the care of ever increasing families. The issue remains, however, of women's contribution to the birth of infants. This is not something men are able to do. What *is* different in the modern period is that women are no longer classified *primarily* as mothers. Being a mother is one of the things women can do. It is not the only, or approved thing.

The point is that feminism has freed women from secondary status as mothers. No longer seen as property in need of protection, women's choices are given as much weight as men's choices in many places.

Biology is part of who we are. How cultures opt to think about that biology is another part of who we are. Rapid shifts in social constructions of gender have been characteristic of our time.

This has been true for men as well as for women, especially among educated classes. Men, once seen as essentially uninvolved with house work or child rearing obligations, have begun taking on both. This is made possible, in part, by the fact that men, especially educated men, increasingly work in the information industry instead of being employed in labor intensive and manufacturing roles. Such a development has enabled them to have more defined work hours and to be thus available for tasks at home and in their families.

The genders have tended to converge in the modern period. Sex roles are less rigid and circumscribed. A breakdown in old fashion morality, so decried by religious fundamentalists, has tended to normalize behaviors and orientations once thought deviant.

What was true on family farms of a few hundred years ago is no longer true in modern interconnected cities. So why should myths that stem from earlier times be helpful in the era of iPhones?

The answer to this question has to do with developed interiority. From our homes in modern cities we continue to read classical literature. We continue to study the history and philosophy of ancient civilizations. We attempt, in short, to broaden our outlooks.

Ours is an age of psychoanalysis and psychology. Psychological understandings of who we are as people have become commonplace—they have demanded attention beyond simply biological focus.

We want to know how we think and feel and who, really, we are. Exploring the foundations of one's self necessarily involves an examination of one's childhood environment. We are products of the contexts of our childhoods: what our parents were like, how they thought, how life was conducted in our houses, what was valued, as well as how we were helped or hindered in our own development.

Abuse and trauma, when present, are life changing events. How was this dealt with? Were we able to talk honestly with our parents, or was this impossible?

In many cases how our parents thought about things is how we were taught to think about things. Our parents created the environment in which we lived and in which we learned about life. What did we learn?

We likely learned we were not quite who our parents thought we were. They may have been close or not close at all. As we grew we gradually developed our own sense of what matters in life—what matters in our own lives. The myths are suggesting this element: coming to know what matters. Such a project entails coming to know what it is you wish to live your life *for*. That is to what will you be most dedicated?

Both Psyche and Parsifal dedicated their lives to endeavors greater than they were. These were dedications both of them discovered. They were not imposed.

Psyche devoted herself to creating the sacred in the realm of the human. That is, through her, she sought to enable the sacred to live. Parsifal devoted himself to providing the energy and awareness that enables life.

Both of these mythic elements exist in all of us. We know this, because they resonate in us. Often one or the other is stronger and urges us in its direction. But because both are human, we may embody both of them. There is a difference between biology and identity.

It is important to understand that neither Psyche nor Parsifal sought power.

One thing these myths are suggesting is that the pursuit of power is a pursuit of the wrong thing. By definition power involves a measure of control over others (Benjamin, 1988).

The modern period has not escaped the human race's long standing lust for power. Yet this power has not always been constructive. When one seeks power over another, one typically seeks to reduce that other person's voice and capability, reserving these things for him or herself. In this sense, power is inherently exploitive.

Exploitation is not in the service of life.

It is only when people are able to see and treat others as equal that life may be maximized. This involves genuine mutual respect.

The quest for power, on the other hand, involves questions of worth. We seek what we do not have. If the only way I can feel myself of worth is to feel myself superior to you, it is clear I have a lack. If I felt truly of worth, I would have no need to profit at your expense.

In many parts of our modern world the entire social and interpersonal fabric is power based. That is, relative positions of power determine in themselves social and interpersonal interactions. In such situations, there is nothing of value beyond power and relative rank. The human dimension is left out. Here, one's power position is seen as one's identity.

It is especially true in the modern period that achievement is part of our daily existence. Achievement, however, is an enterprise that need not involve a lust for power. The difference lies in the motivation one has.

I may study hard for an exam with the intent of doing as well as I possibly can. I may not seek to outdo everyone else. Presumably they are each trying to do as well as they can too. Thus we are all trying to do a similar thing. We are a group that took the exam and tried to do as best we could.

We may, of course, be ranked according to how well we did, but this is a ranking of scores. It is not a ranking of the worth we have as human beings. Worth for being a human being comes from a different place than test scores.

Worth as a human being comes from being thought of and treated as a person of worth. That is, regardless of test scores, our worth remains. A terrible person may attain a high score, and, conversely, a wonderful person may score poorly.

We live in a society that overvalues achievement and success. It tends to value these things over human worth. In such a society it is easy to get lost and disoriented. It is only by realizing there is a difference between one's achievements and one's worth that sanity may prevail. Being worthwhile does not mean being superior, just as being ordinary does not mean being worthless.

What is understood and felt to be human is different from appearance. Modern Facebook culture may swing entirely on appearance, but who we are in our lives does not. Further, appearance, when it is dissevered from genuine identity, necessarily involves power and manipulation. Regardless of how it may appear, reality remains what it is. Rain falls down, people are born and die, and we each live our lives focused toward something.

The myths are suggesting that at a basic level we are people who must come to some sort of terms with life. In this sense our destinies are in our own hands. Whether we are lost in the woods like Parsifal or lost in limbo like Psyche, we each must find our way through.

What will we use as a guide?

Psychological health involves the discovery of who one is, how one's personality is constructed, as well as why one sees the world they way one does. This involves a different perspective than one is able to have simply from one's own assumptions.

Since parents and teachers are not perfect, distortions creep into one's developmental environment. The therapeutic discovery and understanding of these distortions allows for the development of a more adequate sense of one's self and the world. One may have had, for example, parents and teachers who relegated one to inferior status. Parents and teachers may have operated in autocratic terms. As a result one may have lived in a power driven environment and assumed therefore the nature of the world was power driven.

Becoming able to understand one's formative environment allows one to move beyond it. That is, what had seemed to be a universal truth now appears to be partial.

In similar fashion, gender wars may have played a significant role in one's background. It is possible to emerge from one's childhood with a grossly distorted picture of gender. One may have, for example, learned women are worthless and men are disasters. One may have had minimal exposure to opposite sex people and therefore have assumed we are alike or so impossibly different we will never possibly understand each other.

This could be a problem, because the power system routinely assigns women a lesser status. Women who don't seek to understand men with men as their source or men who don't seek to understand women with women as their source are required to fall back on assumptions and stereotypes. In extreme cases empathy between these groups may be impossible.

Raised apart as genders, for the most part, our understanding of each other is made difficult. This in turn makes it more difficult to put oneself in the place of a person from a different gender. One's background may have held genders to be either narrowly or widely different. Indeed one's experiences may have been almost entirely with one sex to the exclusion of the other.

Assuming another person's life is less important than one's own is a recipe for maladjustment. Obviously a social impetus to see individuals in terms of differential worth, along with exclusionary practices, does not improve resonant well-being.

In attachment theory it is thought important how the mother holds the infant in her mind. In other words the infant must be able to find him or herself in the mind of the mother. This requires a resonant empathy between the two which is called bonding.

In a similar fashion, it is an important question how we hold other people in our minds. The person they find in our minds will influence their behavior. In this we can either serve the forces of growth or destruction. That is we can seek to help others grow or seek power over them.

The myths of Psyche and Parsifal argue for a commitment to growth. At a fundamental level they suggest that it is this commitment and focus that is the hope for a truly human race.

PART IV

The oddly difficult task of shifting the context is what opens a life to a greater perspective. It solves, if you will, the restricted life.

Pope Francis spoke about avoiding the "stubbornness and the 'idolatry' of "closed ways of thinking."

> ...there is a dictatorship of a narrow line of thought" which kills "people's freedom, their freedom of conscience. This is the drama of the closed heart, the drama of the closed mind, and when the heart is closed, this heart closes the mind, and when the heart and mind are closed there is no place for God. It is a closed way of thinking that is not open to dialogue, to the possibility that there is something else, the possibility that God speaks to us, tells us about His journey, as he did to the prophets. These people did not listen to the prophets and did

not listen to Jesus. It is something greater than a mere stubbornness. No, it is more: it is the idolatry of their own way of thinking. 'I think this, it has to be this way, and nothing more'. These people had a narrow line of thought and wanted to impose this way of thinking on the people of God. Jesus rebukes them for this: 'You burden the people with many commandments, and you do not touch them with your finger (Blumberg, 2014).'

The task of crossing the line from what is known to what lies beyond what is known is required for significant psychotherapy. That is, one must *surrender* to the process. In psychotherapy one tells one's own version of who one is and the life one has had. The therapist or analyst, who by definition is across the line, as he or she is different from oneself, listens to these accounts and tries to understand them.

He or she may ask questions. He or she may attempt to fill in missing parts. He or she will have an experience of me while I talk. That is, he or she will learn how it feels to be in my presence. I will have assumptions about the therapist or analyst which will be discussed. I will, in short, have the experience of being with someone who is "other," but who is doing all they can to hear me.

In this process, I will experience a bit of what it is like to be beyond myself. That is, I will experience not how I look to myself, but how I look to another. When my story is told back to me, if that telling is empathic and accurate enough, I will be able to see why it is a limited story of a limited existence. I will, in essence, begin to have a sense of that story in *its wider context*.

I will, if you will, be the fish who experiences not-water and so is able to have a different sense of what water is.

In therapeutic settings such as Brad Reedy's *Evoke Therapy Programs* the shift in context is even clearer). Its wilderness therapy program for troubled youth, for example, focuses on teenagers who have come from their known context to the program, which is in the Utah wilderness. Thus, there is a dramatic and profound shift in context. Further, in the wilderness comfort and survival is able to be attained only by group effort. People must pull together or there will be no shelter in severe conditions. There will be no warm food, or adequate living conditions, &c.

Therapists and counselors in this program are not like parents in that they want to hear the feelings of residents. They want to help residents succeed. They will listen to anything.

The point is that old problematic patterns don't work in the new context—they are actually counter-productive.

Therapists and counselors don't demand compliance. In the wilderness it is not compliance that works, it is survival. And when a group pulls together to survive it is a major achievement, one of which anyone could be proud.

A difficult juncture then is the return to the original context at the end of the program. Hopefully the teenager will have had sufficient experience of his or her own achievement as well as the experience of being heard and not judged that he or she will *not* now be able to re-enter and take up the same role he or she had in the home matrix. This will upset the status quo of the home environment. It too will have to grow.

Having been to another context and succeeded there, the teenager will be able to view and experience home as being only one place in a world of many places. It may even not be the best place.

Also in significant psychotherapy or psychoanalysis one gradually is able to experience one's background in a similar way—as one place in a world of many places. One is more able to see the strengths and weaknesses of one's background and can therefore begin to understand how that background contributed to the ways one is today. The story begins to make sense.

In such situations it is not uncommon to find the part one had to play in one's life is a part demanded by others and not a part that comes from one's own individual truth. Thus one is not who one has been taught one was. And since the therapist or analyst doesn't need me to play the old part, I am free to *discover* and be who I more authentically realize myself to be.

In this sense, the crossing of the border experience allows for the birth of a new kind of life, a life not possible in the old matrix.

Routinely significant defensive structures and patterns stand in the way of any attempt I make to move--or even consider change. The context is opposed.

Another problem is that while I have developed in my old context, so has my neurobiology. That is to say, I have wired to the old context. It has been, if you will, the "world" to which I have developed both behavioral and neurobiological responses. I am literally a creature of that world.

Finding myself in a new context or world, both my neurobiology and myself find ourselves in a place for which we are ill prepared. Not having been here before we have no learning or wiring upon which to rely. In fact, it is quite the opposite. Almost everything I know as well as almost all my wiring is patterned on the world where now I am not. Thus my training and wiring keep trying to *correct* me back to the old patterns—because that is now we have always survived.

My students in Oregon told me that if the barn catches on fire, and you get the horses out, you must tie them up. If you don't, they will run back in the barn and perish. Why? They have learned the barn is the *safe place*. It is not safe today, but they have no way to comprehend that.

Similarly, we require support while we learn to cope with a different sort of life. Just as one doesn't learn to play the piano in a day, so one doesn't adjust to a new life in a day. It takes a good deal of practice and experience.

Whether or not we return to the old context, or to what-ever degree, we will not be the same person who left. Our accounts will meet ears from a different base. It will be a bit like rock and roll concerts. We say, "You had to be there."

And it will be important that we keep on going. There is yet a universe that lies beyond our new found expansion. It doesn't end.

For all these reasons crossing the line is the *essential* element in transformation.

A note of caution must be stressed. The process of cross-ing the line to the greater experience requires a genuine sur-render to the unknown. This is why fear so often stops the crossing.

There are people who travel the world, go to school, study religion, have children, attend art galleries, and still-- in a core sense--never leave home. That is they continue to think of themselves as inhabiting the identity of their earli-est training.

But since they have done all the "enlightenment things," they feel they have crossed the line to greater awareness. The problem is all of their experience has been compatible and understandable within the terms of their original con-text--as if that original context is a true basis for the world.

Until the original context becomes only one small section of a multi-contextual world, one has not truly become a citizen of that multi-contextual world, and one remains grounded where one began.

PART V

The discovery that the world's myths are essentially telling the same story is remarkable. It is the human story. Again, the human story consists of what I know and what lies beyond what I know—and the requirement to discover the latter.

But below this story, at a more fundamental level, lies language. The story is told with language. Thus language is prior. It is language that is the essential human element. It becomes profoundly obvious that language has the same configuration of significance that our lives do.

In fact language may be considered the essential human element *par excellence*.

This insight may be clearly seen in the work of Wittgenstein (1953) and Gadamer (1976) among others.

In his memoir of Wittgenstein, Malcolm (1954) stated:

One day when Wittgenstein was passing field where a football game was in progress the thought first struck him that in language we play games with words. A central idea of his philosophy, the notion of 'language-game', apparently had its genesis in this incident (p. 65).

Wittgenstein's thought may be stated as follows:

[For Wittgenstein]...words are not pictures, but pieces used in various language-games. And just as the significance of a piece in chess depends on its "role in the game" (PI, sect. 563) —i.e., how it can be moved, how one behaves with it—so the meaning of a word is its role in the various language-games in which it figures, the kind of behavior that surrounds its use, the kind of behavior in which its use is embedded. An expression only has meaning in—indeed only gets its meaning from—these modes of behavior...(Malcolm p. 93).

An expression has meaning only in the stream of life (Pitcher, p. 244).

The consequence of this reasoning is that meaning is a function of *use*. One discovers the meaning by understanding the use. And use, of course, is a form of behavior. But it is not behavior in the abstract by any means. It is behavior that occurs within a specific or individual context. In an important sense, it is the context in which the behavior occurs and the behavior together that determine meaning. The behavior and the context cannot be 'meaningfully" separated.

Thus a statement in an ambiguous context may not be understandable. It becomes understandable when the context is clarified—not when the word is (arbitrarily) defined.

An example is the following from a local newspaper columnist (Kirby, 2014).

> We took Walter out to the desert and shot him.

This statement becomes understandable when we learn that Walter is a black powder canon that shoots bowling balls. That is to say we need to know the context to make sense of the statement.

If for no other reason, it is critical for the analyst or therapist to understand as much as possible about the context in which a patient lives, thinks, feels, and understands in order to make sense of his or her behavior, including which language-games he or she plays.

Just as there is no universal person, so there is no universal language-game, and thus there is no universal truth. An individual person and an individual context differ from all others.

The point is thus that membership in a class is achieved via language and analogy, not essence. There is no thing all women have in common. No thing all jewelry, all broken hearts, all baseballs, &c., have in common. They are related by the language-game that is used in a specific instance concerning them. And all language-games have, at best, a family resemblance.

According to Wittgenstein:

> We thought we were describing the world, but what we were really describing were the window panes through which we see the world.

Before these suggestions were understood, the language was typically overrun in focusing on that which the language described, suggested, posited, &c.

Then suddenly knowing had much more to do with language than it did with things.

Freud observed:

> Civilization began the first time an angry person cast a word instead of a rock (Kehl, 2005)

According to postmodernism, one of the reasons for this is that things are a construction in the first place and dependent upon language for their understanding in the second. Postmodernists argue that thought is irreducibly linguistic; it can be practiced only in and through historical and context-dependent "language-games" or "discourses"...There is no reality for us outside such systems because, as Rorty argued:

> "there is no way to think about either the world or our purposes except by using language"...All language-games generate their own rules about how to play, what counts as a successful move, and so forth. But by definition these rules are context dependent and valid only within a particular game. Games and their rules are incommensurable. (see Flax, 2000, p. 202)

In light of such concepts, Foucault (1994) undertook what he called "An Archaeology of the Human Sciences." He looked at scientific papers from the past several hundred years. What he found was scarcely an objective study. He found the questions asked, the experiments conceived, the data considered, and the interpretation of those data were each heavily influenced by the times and the cultural conditions during which such experiments took place. That is, social issues influenced what was thought, discovered, and understood.

Heisenberg noted:

> The common division of the world into subject and object, inner world and outer world, body and soul, is no longer adequate and leads us into difficulties (Kehl, 2005, p. 63).

This kind of study ushered in postmodernism and also drove a nail in notions of universal truths and essential certainties. It meant what one saw was importantly colored by where one stood.

An example of this in terms of the study of gender was offered by Fausto-Sterling (2000). (Dr. Fausto-Sterling is a research biologist at Brown University.)

> Individual scientists are inclined to believe one or another claim about biology based in part on scientific evidence and in part on whether the claim confirms some aspects of life that seems personally familiar...[for example] labeling someone a man or a woman is a social decision. We may use scientific knowledge to help us make the decision, but only our beliefs about gender—not science—can define our sex. Furthermore, our beliefs about gender affect what kinds of knowledge scientists produce about sex in

the first place...*Our bodies are too complex to provide clear-cut answers about sexual difference.* The more we look for a simple physical basis for "sex," the more it becomes clear that "sex" is not a pure physical category. What bodily signals and functions we define as male or female come already entangled in our ideas about gender (pp ix, 4, and 5). (My italics.)

Thus what I see and know is constructed from what I am able to find and is carried on the language I am able to use.

The constructs that come to be commonly accepted at any time and in any place are more the result of the operations of power than they are of accuracy or "truth."

I construct a sense of myself in the interpersonal context of my family, all members of which have their own constructs of me. Thus my construction is influenced by its context.

When I seek a therapist, I meet with a person who seeks to develop his or her own construct of me that is hopefully based on some theoretical understanding (itself a construct). He or she will then attempt to learn about my own construct of myself. We will develop constructs of each other—and of the relationship we have created and maintain (the "analytic third").

Still, hopefully in there somewhere, we will both find ways to construct things differently. This gives us a chance to experience things differently and hopefully to discover a more workable world in which to function—as well as a more effective construct of self.

That is to say, we together will need to find another way to describe and therefore be able to experience the material we consider. It may have been an unspoken truth, for example, that my parents were shy and afraid of the world. Speaking this truth allows for a different perspective. Similarly I may have thought all people essentially fear others, and I may be able to discover this is not the case. Thus the world can appear as a very different place to me.

Further it is due to this active interaction between myself and the context that a view is possible in the first place.

Language is the tool that conceptually separates as well as unites things. We are all excited when the child uses a word correctly (what we often call "learning the names of things"). In order to use the word "chair" correctly, the child must know the floor, or her foot is not part of the chair. That is, she must know a bit about what a chair is and what it is not. The word "chair" may be correctly used to describe this object. It may not correctly be used to describe the floor as well.

If the child insists on calling the chair "banana," we correct her. That is not a correct use of the language. The child learns the language by using the language correctly in a context. The language, if you will, makes the context intelligible.

This is also true of thoughts themselves. Thoughts are formed from language and become intelligible by being described.

D.T. Suzuki, the Zen master, said:

The contradiction so puzzling to the ordinary way of thinking comes from the fact that we have to use language to communicate our inner experience which in its very nature transcends linguistics (Kehl, 2005).

This seems to be such an easily understandable comment, as so many of our experiences seem to have a dimension that lies beyond our thoughts or our descriptions in much the same way the chair lies beyond the word.

Suzuki is likely thinking about direct experience or transcendent moments. Of course neither direct experience nor transcendent feelings can be fully captured in language any more than can the chair.

But especially with regard to emotional matters, description may not be the most effective route to take. Here, it may be preferable to *evoke* the emotion or the experience. This requires the use of metaphor instead of descriptive language.

As Campbell observed:

Every religion is true one way or another. It is true when understood metaphorically. But when it gets stuck in its own metaphors, interpreting them as facts, then you are in trouble (1988, p. 56).

Metaphor is the linguistic device for articulating experiences and thoughts beyond the capacity of description.

If we had not developed metaphor we would only have history. That is, we would have a description of human life, but we would not have the feeling part—what it *meant* to be there. That is, much of what is most important about us is carried in metaphors and evocative language. It is, if you will, the language of the heart, instead of the language of the head (these are themselves metaphors).

It is in this way the ancient myths were able to be so important. They were metaphorical ways to talk about what mattered most. In a sense, they were the first psychology and allowed understanding in a world not understandable in other ways.

Therefore, if you think about it, metaphor allowed us as people to cross the line from a life of facts alone to a world of meaning and great emotional range. Crossing this line is what enabled us to be human.

Dr. Freud once observed:

Everywhere I go I find that a poet has been
there before me (Kehl, 2005).

This recalls Hamilton (1940) who claimed the person
thought closest to the Gods in Ancient Greece was the poet
instead of the priest.

This may be thought to be the case, because it is the poet
who is constantly creating things that are new. In this
project, he or she is akin to the psychoanalyst. Both are
constantly crossing borders in the search for new perspectives.

PART VI

Consider a comic example. It too represents what is other, a new country.

A group of teenagers was asked to interpret a series of classic paintings. Below is a series of the paintings and the interpretations given (see C).

Esther Before Ahasuerus
Franz Caucig

Esther just found out there's no Wi-Fi in this palace.

Alcibiades Being Taught by Socrates
Francois-Andre Vincent

Alcibiades is lookin' all swag in his rad new outfit, but Socrates is all, "No son of mine is gonna be seen in public dressed like some gangster rapper. Change into those totally lame clothes I bought you from Wal-Mart right now!"

Don Juan
Lord Byron

Don's sayin', "Yo girl, lemme touch your boob." And she's like, "Of course, Jason. Anything for you."

Paradise
Lucas Cranach the Elder

The naked dude's all, "Yo, old man, you know where the Taco Bell at?" Fancy robe guy is like, "It's over there."

The Parnassus
Raphael

Apollo's busting out his acoustic fiddle at this really chill party and everyone else is all, "Come on, bro. Don't be *that* guy."

Young Woman With Unicorn
Raphael

Girl's got this bitchin' tiny unicorn, but she's all sad and stuff because she's totally spoiled and wanted an iPhone 5 instead.

The question is: why are these funny?

Clearly the context in which the teenagers live is not wide enough to include that of classical painting. It, rather, includes what the teenagers know. Consequently, the teenagers interpret the world in terms of what they know. What else can they do?

Similarly, the world of the classical painters knows nothing of the context of the teenagers. Why should it?

The point is, of course, we are as blind as the teenagers— and the painters. *And* our interpretations are equally stupid. To solve this shortsighted situation, we must widen our vision. That is, we must move to a new vantage point.

PART VII

The synoptic Gospel According to St. John begins this way:

> In the beginning was the Logos, and the Logos was with God, and the Logos was God (see A).

Awareness was thus the "light that shineth into the darkness." It is awareness that allows me to understand the world around me. It is also awareness that allows me to understand myself.

Like other kinds of tools, however, understanding requires constant attention. If the essential ingredient in what is meaningful is contrast, our understanding requires constant refreshing by crossing from the context in which it is operating to the context which is beyond that.

Nothing can be meaningful that cannot be done wrong. If the word "chair" could be used to describe anything whatsoever, it would be meaningless. And while no experience of the sacred is adequately describable, it too has meaning in light of what it is and is not.

The implications of this is that in order to be able to grasp what is, one must also be able to grasp what "what is" is not. That is, one must know what "is" as well as what "is not."

I cannot understand my own situation unless I can move beyond it.

The ancient truths worked on this principle. What the ancients thought most important was the development of the ability to see what lay beyond the present. Seeing beyond the present required the courage to face the darkness. Crossing into that darkness was the secret to life.

Psychotherapy of any significant sort also requires the courage to face the darkness about oneself (i.e., that which lies beyond what I know). One must give up control and allow oneself to have a different kind of experience. This new experience is the element that allows one to develop a new point of view, so one can see oneself and one's world from a different place.

The results of this transformation are profound and life changing. One has crossed over to being able to know what one could not possibly have known before.

It is that crossing that makes us human.

REFERENCES

A. http://www.bibleresearcher.com/logos.html

B. http://www.snwp.com

C. http://themetapicture.com/when-modern-teenagers-interpret-classic-art/

Benjamin, J. The Bonds of Love: Psychoanalysis, Feminism, and the Problem of Domination. Pantheon. 1988.

Blumberg, A. Pope Francis: Only An Open Mind Can Bring The Faithful Close To God." Huffington Post, 04-11-14.

Bulfinch, T. Bulfinch's Mythology [Cupid and Psyche]. Avenel. 1929.

Campbell, J. The Hero With A Thousand Faces. Bollingen/ Princeton, 1949.

Campbell, J. The Inner Reaches of Outer Space. Harper. 1986.

Campbell, J. The Power of Myth. Doubleday. 1988

Campbell, J. Transformations of Myth Through Time. Harper. 1990.

Cavell, S. Must We Mean What We Say? Cambridge. 2002.

de Troyes, C. Arthurian Romances: Including Perceval. Everyman. 1987.

Eliad, M. The Sacred and the Profane. Harcourt. 1957.

Fausto-Sterling, A. Sexing the Body. Basic. 2000.

Flax, J. Thinking Fragments: Psychoanalysis, Feminism, and Postmodernism in the Contemporary West. California. 1990.

Foucault, M. The Order of Things. Vintage. 1970.

Gadamer, H-G. Philosophical Hermeneutics. Ed and trans: P.C. Smith. Yale. 1976.

Hamilton, E. Mythology. Mentor. 1940.

Kehl, R. Love Letters to the Universe. Darling. 2005.

Kirby, R. "Walter The Bowling Ball Howitzer Did Us Proud." Salt Lake Tribune. 04-07-2014.

Malcolm, N. Ludwig Wittgenstein: A Memoir. Oxford. 1958.

Mitchell, S.A. Influence and Autonomy in Psychoanalysis. Analytic Press. 1997.

Neumann, E. Amor and Psyche. Harper. 1956.

Pitcher, G. The Philosophy of Wittgenstein. Prentice-Hall. 1964.

Rorty, R. Philosophy and the Mirror of Nature. Princeton. 1979.

Wittgenstein, L. Philosophical Investigations. Macmillan, 1953.

Wittgenstein, L. The Blue and Brown Books. Harper. 1958.

ABOUT THE AUTHOR

J.D. Gill is a clinical psychologist at the University of Utah. She is an Adjunct Associate Professor of Psychology, a Clinical Professor of Counseling Psychology, and an Adjunct Associate Professor of Psychiatry in the University of Utah School of Medicine. Dr. Gill maintains a busy practice at the University of Utah Neuropsychiatric Institute.

Dr. Gill has degrees in English Literature, Philosophy, Psychology, and two post docs in psychoanalytic psychotherapy. She studied in the Writing Program at the University of Utah. She has been a practicing psychologist for over forty years and has presented over five hundred seminars, lectures, workshops, and papers. A world traveler, Dr. Gill has actively sought to experience multiple viewpoints and perspectives.

www.ingramcontent.com/pod-product-compliance
Lightning Source LLC
Chambersburg PA
CBHW071359310526
45790CB00019B/1554